Cite Your Sources

A MANUAL FOR DOCUMENTING FAMILY HISTORIES AND GENEALOGICAL RECORDS

by
Richard S. Lackey
Fellow, American Society of Genealogists

Introduction by Winston DeVille

UNIVERSITY PRESS OF MISSISSIPPI
Jackson, Mississippi

Library of Congress Cataloging-in-Publication Data

Lackey, Richard S.
     Cite your sources.

     Includes index.
     1. Genealogy—Handbooks, manuals, etc. 2. Bibli-
ographical citations—Handbooks, manuals, etc.
I. Title.
CS16.L3 1985   929'.1   85-20371
ISBN 0-87805-286-0

*Printed and bound in the
United States of America*

FOREWORD

The purpose of this manual is to provide genealogists with an uncomplicated, yet academically acceptable guide to basic citations. It has been prepared with the needs of genealogists foremost in mind and represents careful consideration based on my own ideas and on those of many respected expert genealogists and historians.

There are other methods of citing sources; this one, however, is the only one designed with the particular needs of genealogists in mind. While I have used many authentic examples based on Southern sources and some ficticious examples, none of the examples should be used for locating actual documents. Genealogists using non-Southern sources will be able to substitute data from other geographical areas with facility, maintaining the principles and components outlined herein. In fact, instructors will, no doubt, find it useful to have students write other examples, using local sources. The table of contents and index should allow anyone to locate information easily and quickly.

This book was written in response to the urgings of students, colleagues, editors, librarians and archivists. I realize the heavy obligations I have incurred; many associates have provided suggestions, advice, valuable criticism, encouragement and help in other ways. Of my debts, the largest are to Winston De Ville, F.A.S.G., of New Orleans; Dr. James R. Johnson of Memphis; and to H. Martin Soward III of Ingleside, Texas. The assistance of these three friends proved invaluable and I sincerely thank them for their friendship and their help. I benefited also from the help of John Frederick Dorman, F.A.S.G., F. Wilbur Helmbold, Etoile Loper Hopkins, C.G.R.S., Donna R. Hotaling, Bill R. Linder, Mary N. Speakman, C.G., Lawrence K. Wells, and Dr. Neil D. Thompson, F.A.S.G. Also, I wish to express my appreciation to Jane P. McManus, CPS, for typing the manuscript.

Most importantly, my loving appreciation goes to my wife, Saralyn, and my daughter, Ellen. Were it not for their patience, help, and encouragement, this work would have never been completed. Often, excellent advice fell on deaf ears; responsibility for errors and deficiencies is solely my own.

Richard S. Lackey, *Fellow*
American Society of Genealogists

Forest, Mississippi
3 April 1980

INTRODUCTION

During the entire course of Western Civilization, genealogy as an institution of academic integrity has never survived. Although the impact of the family has always been felt in general society, in politics, economics, science, and in so many other areas of life, the purity and consistency of scholarship on the subject historically are irregular. In Europe, England, and in other parts of the world, genealogy traditionally became the exclusive domain of the upwardly mobile and socially ambitious, too often without regard to authentically documented lineages.

Probably as a consequence, during the early years in America, few serious studies for family history were produced. Many of our American ancestors were only recently free of the burdens of the common man in the Old World and probably cynical of anything relating to a subject so closely associated with the upperclass, royalty, and the nobility. Too, they were preoccupied with taming a wilderness frontier — and rarely is genealogy expressed in frontier literature. Indeed, recording family history formally is one of the last pursuits of a developing affluent society. Genealogy began to flourish in America, then, not until the prosperous times of the nineteenth century. During its last golden age, however — a century ago — as a serious and well established profession or avenue of learning, genealogy had progressed in scholarship very little since earlier times in mother-countries.

Happily, today, after almost five hundred years in a New World, inquiry into genealogy has stimulated again the public mind. At no point in history has our chosen work had a better opportunity to establish itself finally as a vital and indispensible tool for humanity's intellectual synthesis and as a rewarding and gratifying leisure activity. Science long ago recognized the importance of genealogy. Historians themselves, long justifiably skeptical, are at last becoming aware of genealogy's potential in serious and definitive studies. Today's facile aids — the computer, microfilm, the quick-copier, and modern libraries filled with more published sources than ever before — all these and more should make research in the last years of the twentieth century more exact, efficient, productive *and readily open to criticism* than ever before.

Only scholarship, standards and stability, then, remain, and only the genealogist can regulate these principles. For perspective, let us observe what the natural growth and development of a true scholarly discipline are as precise and measureable as the standards by which serious studies produced by that discipline are judged. If we believe that genealogy is, in fact, a discipline, standards must be set high enough to contain the implied bases or principles. It is a fact that one of the most important of these standards is *proper citation of sources*; the very frame on which written scholarship hangs is *precise* and *consistent documentation*.

Serious genealogists, wishing to encourage excellence in research and writing, should consider, with the keenest sort of introspection, that as a discipline today, genealogy must try to reflect accurate concepts of the subject on its broadest levels, with practical guidelines, such as Mr. Lackey's present work, for the nonprofessional, nonscholar, or genealogical hobbyist, yet with standards high enough to satisfy the most inquisitive critic. This manual, then, is a milestone in the development of genealogy as a viable field of study. It will be indispensable for teaching genealogical writing techniques in the classroom and will serve all genealogists who strive to produce well - documented family histories.

Clearly, the time has passed when genealogy had to depend on its sister disciplines for formulating standards, setting goals, judging peers, coordinating internal harmony and mutual aid, and for establishing firmly the study of family history in the academic sphere. If genealogy is, in fact, a discipline, it is, by definition, *self-disciplinary*. I am convinced that reputable genealogists are capable of accepting and executing the responsibilities inherent in this definition. All we require now are the exciting visions of genealogy's growth, development, and on-going contributions to knowledge.

Winston De Ville, *Fellow*
American Society of Genealogists

New Orleans
8 May 1980

CONTENTS

PART I
DOCUMENTING RESEARCH

PART II
CITATION FORMS

PART III

SHORT OR SECOND USE OF NOTES

PART I

DOCUMENTING RESEARCH

CITING SOURCES
ACCORDING TO STANDARD FORM

As other distinct disciplines have developed standard styles acceptable in their fields for presenting and documenting written research results, likewise, genealogists should also have standard forms of citations which meet their special needs. Quite possibly the reason many genealogists have neglected to use available style sheets and manuals prepared for general use is that genealogists do indeed have special needs. It is time for all genealogists to consider adopting an acceptable reference form or style for citing the records commonly used in the field. This is the purpose of this book.

Genealogical notes should always be retained in written form. No knowledgeable genealogist would ever undertake an investigation of a family with the idea of committing records and sources to memory. Every single person engaged in the fascinating search for ancestors will necessarily, at some point, be faced with the problems of completing a written account which documents research results. Citing sources has been the primary area of frustration for many.

Each year, genealogists spend thousands of dollars attending lectures and buying publications designed to direct them to some desired source of needed information. Speakers, teachers, and authors never fail to emphasize the importance of recording accurate information. While most genealogical educators stress the importance of recording the source of all information collected, few, if any, suggest how that task should be accomplished. Therefore, too often we find expertly abstracted records and are informed that the source was "The Census" or "Marriage Records." Many lay-people have become experts in locating and abstracting obscure genealogical records. Any person who can properly learn to abstract a document can also learn properly to cite it so that another interested researcher can quickly and easily locate the record. For the results of our efforts at research to be useful to others in this or in future generations, such citations are absolutely required.

It must be pointed out that no circumstances whatsoever exempt any genealogist from providing documentation according to an acceptable form. This writer has heard it said: "That genealogist was a preacher," in a tone that would defy anyone to question credibility of work. Further, this writer has seen undocumented genealogical work produced by an individual proclaiming "a master's degree in library science," "a doctorate in school administration," and "a position of county clerk for thirty-five years." Achievement in another field does not ensure proficiency in the field of genealogy. No person, no matter what his station, should decide that his credibility rank eliminates the need for standard documentation of genealogical work.

For some unknown reason, beginning genealogists seem to think that if a few notes — no matter the form — are provided, then their work is "documented" or "proved." Others, with years of research experience, think that so-called "obvious sources," such as "The Federal Census" or "Territorial Papers," need no documentation. Such thinking has resulted in much poorly documented work. Just because "The Family Bible" is in Mother's trunk, such a reference will have no meaning to a stranger or a reader in future years. Further, the "obvious source" used by genealogists in one state may be totally unknown to the most knowledgeable genealogist working with sources in another state. In short, all arguments against use of standard forms by genealogists are invalid.

Not every genealogist is interested in submitting work to a journal, completing a book, or even in completing a compiled genealogy. Every genealogist should, however, want the results of his work to be useful even if maintained only in organized note form. Thus, every person seriously engaged in genealogical research has a vested interest in developing some standard form of suitable written citation of documents.

Almost every genealogist wishes to emphasize the accuracy with which his records were compiled. In the preface of a book, one author reported that efforts to ensure accuracy in every detail resulted in "a stiff neck." Another writer reported that "photo copies of every record were purchased to ensure that no errors were made." Statements such as these become unnecessary if genealogical records are documented according to standard form. Most expert genealogists can readily evaluate the extent and worth of one's efforts and work by simply looking at the documentation. The following notes are actual "documentations" seen by this writer:

EXAMPLES OF
NONSTANDARD AND UNACCEPTABLE FORMS

--"Reference material collected by my friend"

--"A big magazine (authorative) on Virginia Volume II, page 109, I think" [sic]

--"A Bible in South Carolina"

--"Deeds of North Carolina, #30 - p.10"

--"A role [sic] of Microfilm sold by the U.S. Govt. and National Archives out of Washington, D.C."

--The Library of Congress"

--"File #19603"

--"Marriage Bond B, Folio 169, Office of the Superior Court, Courthouse"

--"The Census Record, 1790 to 1880"

--"A book by James in the Mobile Library, pages 160-168 (our line)"

--"DAR records and Mormon Records (both are accurate)"

--"S. Micro-film of Civil War Men"

--"Pages 120-127 by Boddie in one of his books named Historical Southern Families"

--"My cousin's book which the DAR takes on pp. 18-19"

--"A History of My Family and Allied Lines, (pages 176-192) by a professional genealogist"

--"Worth S. Ray, N.C. (old Albemarle) He wrote only true books"

--"A death certificate written by the State"

It is not possible to make use of any of the notes given above — although they have been selected from genealogical reports, compilations, letters and articles. Should anyone ask why a standard form of citation is needed in the field of genealogy? It should be noted that, although the notes above have been selected as examples of poor and meaningless citations, a few were included in work done by individuals offering to do research for others for a fee. References such as these readily identify the untrained genealogist and provide modern researchers with valid reasons to question and discredit the total value of such work. Today, it takes more than a college degree, community standing or a written assurance of excellence to convince most people of the credibility of a genealogy. It takes documentation according to standard form!

GOALS

This writer once found it a sad duty to inform a friend that years of research efforts were virtually worthless because none of the sources of information had been recorded. The friend commented: "I am just doing this for the children, so I don't need to document my work." Any genealogist can tell you that such an admonishment usually means that the person does not know *how* to document his work, and that he hopes no knowledgeable or critical reader will ever have an opportunity to review it. But most people will usually at least recognize the importance of documentation.

Any serious genealogical pursuit is, by its very nature, a scholarly endeavor. Documentation of sources is a distinguishing characteristic of scholarly work. Since most people are engaged in genealogical research simply for personal enjoyment, some never associate such a pleasurable activity with scholarship. Is there any valid reason why a scholarly study cannot be fun? No, none at all!

A few inexperienced researchers will complain that learning to use standard forms of documentation is frustrating and that it really doesn't make any difference whether such things as the author's full name and other standard notetaking components are given. Insistence on exactness of notes is no different than requiring exactness of abstracts. Once the genealogist has mastered documentation, freedom to spend time on other important things will follow. Never again will there be need for a genealogist's request for "the green book" or "the grey box of letters." Librarians and archivists will soon become your best friends!

Genealogists do have different goals. Some simply wish to provide the family with useful genealogical data. Others wish to complete an application required by a lineal organization. Many desire to compile and publish a genealogy and in that manner contribute to the literature in the field. The need to document information and cite sources in standard form is, however, common to all genealogists without regard to goals.

On the other hand, some genealogists have no desire to complete a compiled genealogy or an application for a lineal organization. How can different genealogists, with goals of creating different types of record collections, make use of standard citations?

Remember that all genealogical investigations represent independent work. A genealogist is one who has the training, the experience, and the ability to employ acceptable methods with the reasoning necessary to determine family relationships by a preponderance of all of the best possible evidence available. A compiled genealogy is nothing more than a composition which summarizes the research results about a limited subject by coherently presenting individual facts as well as evaluations and conclusions. A critical reader will simply not accept anyone's work without knowing the evidence upon which it is based. The only way to have work widely accepted is to document it properly.

THE USE OF REFERENCE NOTES

While the primary purpose of reference notes is to provide authority and credibility to the information presented, the researcher should consider the overall use of notes. A variety of notes can be used to make genealogical work meaningful. The genealogist should have a clear understanding of the use of notes so as to achieve desired results. The basic uses follow:

1. To cite the exact source of information.
2. To make cross references to information.
3. To explain, add information, and make statements which amplify the text or

cited source.

4. To make acknowledgements.

1. CITE THE SOURCE USED

Researchers should always cite the *specific* source examined by the researcher. This is one of the most important rules governing the documentation of genealogical sources. However, this apparently simple requirement can become a major pitfall to some genealogists. To state it another way: a researcher may report only that which is *personally* examined. Any reference must reflect the exact form in which the researcher *personally* found the source.

This writer has stated in a published article on sources that genealogical information is, like oil and gas, located where it is found. If information is found in Saudi Arabia, do not report that it was found in Texas. Too many genealogists feel compelled to indicate or infer that the source of their information was a personally-examined original document when, in fact, it was a published abstract or the contribution of a generous correspondent. *The exact source of information should always be given.* This should be done without exception!

This point is so important to proper documentation that the following specific example is

11

given. A genealogist may have the following statement: "By 29 December 1718, Ann Ferguson, the mother of Isabell Ferguson, had become the wife of Robert Bell." An acceptable source for the information is the will of Henry Woodnot. However, the individual researcher preparing a reference to this will should be exact as to the specific record. If "pay dirt" came in the form of a letter from a cousin in Osyka, Mississippi, don't report that it came directly from Will Book "B." Such an untruthful reference is also incorrect form. References to the genealogical statement made above might vary considerably depending on the exact source of information used by that individual researcher. Here are some proper examples:

EXAMPLES

[1]J. Bryan Grimes, Abstracts of North Carolina Wills (Raleigh: E. M. Uzzell & Co., 1910), p. 421.

[2]J.R.B. Hathaway, "Abstracts of Wills," North Carolina Historical and Genealogical Register, I (Oct. 1900), p. 514.

[3]"Will of Henry Woodnot(t)," Records of the Secretary of State, Wills 1712-1722, Bk. 2, p. 176, N.C. Division of Archives and History, Raleigh.

[4]Personal letter referring to the

1718 Will of Henry Woodnot of N.C.,
received by the author from John Doe,
P.O. Box 181, Osyka, Miss., 26 Nov. 1963.

Obviously, the reference which indicates
that the researcher personally examined the offici-
ally recorded will of Henry Woodnot would be judged
as the best possible source for the statement made.
However, the proper and best possible reference for
the individual researcher is the one which reflects
exactly the source personally examined. It is usually impossible for every researcher personally to
examine the best source for every statement made
in a written genealogical presentation. The genealogist who learns to distinguish between "best possible source" and "best possible reference" will
understand and follow the rule of always citing the
exact source of information.

Many times a genealogist needs to cite a
reference taken from a source other than the original. For example, one may wish to cite a published
source found quoted and cited in another published
source. The original may be unavailable so it be-
comes necessary to refer to a published source.

EXAMPLE

[1]Frederic C. Jaher, "Businessmen
and Gentlemen: Nathan and Thomas Gold

Appleton — An Exploration in Intergenerational History," Vol. IV of _Explorations in Entrapreneurial History_ (1966), 17-38 in James R. McGovern, _Yankee Family_ (New Orleans: Polyanthos, 1975), p. i.

It should be perfectly clear to the reader that the reference is to the Jaher article and not to a statement by McGovern. Further, the researcher has not directly consulted the article in original form but is simply taking what is given in the researcher's source, _Yankee Family._

2. MAKE CROSS REFERENCES TO INFORMATION

In his excellent book, _Genealogical Evidence: A Guide to the Standard of Proof Relating to Pedigrees, Ancestry, Heirship and Family History,_ noted genealogist Noel C. Stevenson, F.A.S.G., makes the strong, valid point that "a pedigree or ancestry is established according to a preponderance or greater weight of the evidence." Further, he adds that a point regarding ancestry should seldom be based on one single source. Because of these facts, the genealogist frequently finds it essential to make cross references to information.

For example, a deed of sale from Thomas Smith and Mary, his wife, may be found and cited. It is possible that the land being sold was inherited by

Mary under the terms of John Doe's will stating:
"My real property shall go to Mary, my daughter."[1]
The will of John Doe may have been previously cited,
so only a cross reference to it would be required.

EXAMPLE

[1]"Deed from Thomas Smith and Mary
to Richard Roe," Deed Bk. III; 368-370,
Office of the Chancery Clerk, Courthouse,
Tiskill, Gulf Co., Miss. Cf. text for
N. 42, *infra*. citing will of John Doe.

A cross reference is in order when two or
more facts are related. Such cross references can
add significantly to the usefulness of one's research results.

The Latin terms, *supra* (above) and *infra*
(below) may be used to direct the reader to the
location of a note cited elsewhere in a work.

EXAMPLE

[1]N. 42, *infra*.

[22]N. 18, *supra*.

3. EXPLAIN, ADD INFORMATION, AND MAKE STATEMENTS WHICH AMPLIFY THE TEXT OR CITED SOURCE

Sometimes it is necessary and helpful to

provide statements which explain or amplify the text or the cited source. A researcher may wish to refer to particular records taken from an indirect source. Such a note allows one to supply the reader (and himself) with the location of the original record (although obtained indirectly), as well as to indicate the exact source used.

EXAMPLE

[1]"Deed from Denis Macklenden to Charles Gavin" (dated 7 Dec. 1703; reg. Jan. 1703/04), Chowan Co., N.C., Deed Bk W-#1, p. 48, as abstracted in Margaret M. Hofmann, Chowan Precinct North Carolina 1696 to 1723 (Weldon, N.C.: Roanoke News Co., 1972), p. 14.

This type of note which refers to a specific document obtained indirectly — not consulted by the researcher — can be quite useful to the genealogist. Harm comes only when the reference stops before the reader is informed that the researcher *must* refer to the source from which it was obtained — as in the previous example, the Hofmann book.

Sometimes, especially when genealogists are consulting published abstracts, references to the location of original documents are useful. Consider the difference in the following notes:

EXAMPLES

[1]Joseph W. Watson, <u>Kinfolks of Edgecombe County, North Carolina, 1788–1855</u> (Durham: The Seeman Printery, Inc. 1969), p. 49.

[2]Edgecombe Co., N.C. Deed Bk. 10 p. 310, noted in Joseph W. Watson, <u>Kinfolks of Edgecombe County, North Carolina, 1788–1855</u> (Durham: The Seeman Printery, Inc. 1969), p. 49.

Both notes refer to the source (the Watson book) actually consulted by the researcher. A reader finding the first note might be left in doubt as to the content of the Watson book. Certainly, the reader would have to examine the book to learn the exact source of the information. Other forms could cite the same information.

EXAMPLE

[1]Joseph W. Watson, <u>Kinfolks of Edgecombe County, North Carolina, 1788–1855</u> (Durham: The Seeman Printery, Inc. 1969), p. 49. Watson cites Edgecombe Co., N.C. Deed Bk. 10, p. 310, and refers to a "Deed of gift from Nathan Mayo to Micajah Mayo, 23 Aug. 1802."

When such information is given simply to amplify or more fully explain, the information is best provided in a content note which would follow

17

the reference to the source actually consulted by the researcher.

Any serious genealogist giving consideration to citing the actual source used will see the advantages of honesty in this area. In the past, some genealogists have cited published abstracts as though the original records were examined. When errors are discovered, those genealogists must acknowledge their deception or explain why they were unable to abstract or interpret original records correctly. When a genealogist uses, evaluates, and cites *published abstracts,* he may be justifiably called upon to defend his judgement on the value and interpretation of the abstracts used — nothing more. Usually, adverse criticism comes to a person based on poor work done. Most researchers find it impossible to consult every record in original form, but for all to be honest in citing the records actually consulted is certainly within the realm of possibility. (And, as noted earlier, it is imperative always to cite the exact source personally consulted.)

Statements which amplify the text can be significant. Such statements might provide a point of observation:

EXAMPLE

Text:

John Doe purchased forty acres described as the NW^4 of the NW^4, Section 1, Township 1 North — Range 2 East (190th Principal Meredian).[1] He ....

----

[1]Richard Roe purchased an adjoining 40 acres (NE^4 of the NW^4, Section 1, T. 1N — R. 2E (190th PM) the same day. Register's Monthly Report, 10 July 1829 Westville (deed) U.S. Land Office, Vol. 4, p. 86, Washington Federal Record Center, Suitland, Md. Microfilm copy owned by author.

Or, the same statement might provoke an opinion note, such as:

EXAMPLE

----

[1]This researcher has visited this land and found no evidence of a house site or cemetery; it is his opinion that the land was purchased for speculation and not as a house site for the John Doe family.

All experienced genealogists realize that it is necessary to weigh or evaluate published sources. Remarks or comments about such an evaluation can add to the utility of the work.

[1]John Doe, Deed Abstracts of River
County, Alabama (Mobile: River City Press,
1950), p. 160. It is apparent that these
abstracts represent work done by a care-
less amateur, and that it is essential to
examine the original records.

[2]Weynette Parks Hauns, Craven Pre-
cinct-County, North Carolina Precinct-
County Court Minutes 1712 thru 1715,
Book I (By the comp., 243 Argonne
Drive, Durham, N.C. 27704, 1978), p. 31.
It is apparent that these copies of court
minutes are expertly and carefully compiled and that examination of original
records is necessary only when some
doubt arises.

4. MAKE ACKNOWLEDGEMENTS

Few genealogical investigations are the re-
sult of the work performed entirely by one person.
Usually, at least some information and assistance
is provided by others. It is not only courteous —
rather, it is proper — to acknowledge the efforts of
associates.

Sometimes a colleague might provide a single
document.

EXAMPLE

[1]"John Weldon to John Rainsford, <u>Lease and Release</u>, 3 May 1794, Edgefield Co., S.C., Deed Bk 11, p. 14. Photocopy supplied by Ann Jones Clayton (Mrs. Ed), Clinton, Miss.

Or, a co-worker might make an entire collection available.

EXAMPLE

[1]Etoile Loper Hopkins (Mrs. Oliver), C.G.R.S., P.O. Box 438, Forest, Miss. 39074, allowed the writer to examine all records relating to her genealogy; several references to useful obscure sources were obtained.

In addition, it is possible that information was obtained during formal meetings.

EXAMPLE

[1]In response to a specific question, Winston DeVille, F.A.S.G., directed this researcher to this source during his lecture on "Louisiana Sources," Houston Genealogical Institute, Houston, Texas, 4 June 1979.

In other words, give credit where credit is due!

PART II

CITATION FORMS

II. CITATION FORMS

THE NOTE ENTRY

Details regarding components in a note entry for (I) Books, Pamphlets, and Monographs; (II) Serials; and (III) Unpublished Documents will follow later. In addition, short or second use of notes will be discussed.

Every entry in all notes contains certain elements, and first citations differ, depending upon the type of source and the factors regarding that source. Certain elements are common to all citations:

PUNCTUATION

The necessary items of basic information are presented as a note by the researcher in proper sequence and with certain punctuation marks. The insertion of punctuation marks in and between elements of a simple book citation is illustrated in the following example:

EXAMPLE

[1]Bill R. Linder, How To Trace Your Family History (New York: Everest House, 1978), p. 10.

More complicated notes may require some additional punctuation. The researcher may generally be guided by standard rules concerning the use of punctuation marks within the body of an entry. Punctuation should be used as a device to clarify meaning.

CAPITALIZATION

Basic rules of English grammar should be followed for capitalization.

ABBREVIATION

Abbreviation should be utilized to save space. Researchers are familiar with the common abbreviations of months and states; these should be used in notes for economy of space. Always be consistent with abbreviations. For example, use standard state abbreviations (Tenn., Miss., Wash.) all the time, or use those used by the United States Postal Service (TN, MS, WA), but never use a combination of the two (TN, Miss., WA). Again, remember to be consistent.

In addition, other widely accepted abbreviations can be used. Always keep in mind that clarity is more important than saving space.

SOME COMMONLY USED ABBREVIATIONS

A.G., Accredited Genealogist
A.D.S., autograph document signed
a.k.a., also known as
A.L.S., autograph letter signed
anon., anonymous
app., appendix
assn., association
B.A., Bachelor of Arts
b., born
bap., baptised
bibliog., bibliography
Bk. (Bks. plural), book(s)
bur., buried
ca. (*circa*) about
C.A.L.S., Certified American Lineage Specialist
C.G., Certified Genealogist
C.G.R.S., Certified Genealogical Record Searcher
cf. *(confer)*, compare
ch., chapter
co., county
col., column
comp. (comps. plural), compiler(s)
d., died
dau., daughter
dept., department
diss., dissertation
doc. (docs. plural), document(s)
e.g. (*exempli gratia*), for example
ed. cit. (*editio citata*), edition cited
ed. (eds. plural), editor(s)
esp., especially
est., estate
etc., (*et cetera*), and so forth
exec., executor
F.A.S.G., Fellow, American Society of Genealogists
facs. (or facsim.), facsimile
fig., figure
fn., footnote
F.N.G.S., Fellow, National Genealogical Society

fol., (fols. plural), folio(s)
hist., history or historian
i.e. (*id est*), that is
ibid. (*ibidem*), in the same place
infra., below
introd., introduction
ills., illustrated or illustrator
jour., journal
J.P., Justice of the Peace
l., line
lib., (*liber*) book
lic., license
loc. cit. (*loco citato*), in the place cited
mag., magazine
MS. (MSS plural), manuscript(s)
M.A., Master of Arts
M.G., Minister of the Gospel
M.S., Master of Science
misc., miscellaneous
N. (NN. plural), note(s)
N.B. (*nota bene*), take notice
N.d., no date
N.n., no name
N.p., no place
N. pag., no pagination
N. pub., no publisher
no., number
op., (*opus*) work
op. cit. (*opere citato*), in the work cited
O.S., Old Style (calendar)
p. (pp. plural), page(s)
par., paragraph
passim, here and there
Ph.D., Doctor of Philosophy
pref., preface
pt. (pts. plural), part(s)
q.v. (*quod vide*), which see
R., Range (legal land description)
R.G., Record Group
rev., revised
rpt., reprint

s.p. (*sine prole*), without issue
sec., section
ser., series
sic, thus
soc., society
supra, above
T., Township (legal land description)
TS., typescript
trans., translator
V. (*verso*), the back (of a page)
v.d., various dates
V.R., vital record
viz. (*videlicet*), namely
vol. (vols. plural), volume(s)
yr., year

Also, the titles of very well-known journals and other publications may be abbreviated in notes. For example, the following are among those that could be abbreviated:

EXAMPLE

NGSQ – <u>National Genealogical Society Quarterly</u>
VG   – <u>The Virginia Genealogist</u>
TAG   – <u>The American Genealogist</u>

Further, the researcher may devise abbreviations for works or sources frequently used after the first full citation. It is best to use "Hereinafter..." preceeding such abbreviations. A first citation to a document in the National Archives and Records Service may read, in part, as in the example below.

EXAMPLE

[1]...National Archives and Records
Service, Washington, D.C., hereinafter,
N.A.

MISCELLANEOUS POINTS

Dates are best written by genealogists using the day, the month, and the year (18 June 1942).

Italicized words in print indicate the words should be underlined in typing or handwriting.

Volume numbers or letters should be given as they are found. (IV, iv, t, a, A, 5-A, AAA).

Periods and commas are placed inside quotation marks. Note that footnote numbers in the text itself follow the quotation marks. (."[8]).

Genealogists may place note numbers within a sentence to refer to a specific fact when two or more facts are given from different sources. (John Doe was born 10 June 1855[1] in River County, Alabama.[2])

Do not consider any source too obvious for a citation, even to an informed reader.

PLACEMENT OF NUMBERS AND INDENTIONS

An arabic numeral should be about a half

space above the line. Never use any punctuation after the numeral. Also, never allow a space between numeral and the first letter of the note. Notes should always be numbered consecutively throughout a division such as a section or chapter of a paper.

Indent from the left margin the first line of each note the same number of spaces as is used to indent paragraphs in the text. Always single space notes, and use a separate line for each note. Double space between notes.

EXAMPLE

[1]Richard S. Lackey, F.A.S.G., Cite Your Sources (New Orleans: Polyanthos, Inc., 1980), p. 20.

[2]*Ibid.*, p. 21.

I. BOOKS, PAMPHLETS, AND MONOGRAPHS

THE ENTRY

Citations for all books, pamphlets, and other monographic publications are designed to identify the reference. A complete *first* reference entry for a book should always include four simple basic information items: A. the author entry, B. the complete title, C. publication facts, and D. page number(s). Proper sequence or order of presenting this information is always maintained even if some items are unnecessary or do not apply. With the exception of the page number(s), the title page of most books should usually provide the information required.

EXAMPLE

[1]Bertram Hawthorne Groene, Tracing Your Civil War Ancestor (Winston-Salem: John F. Blair, 1973), pp. 17-19.

A. Author Entry. Most books, pamphlets, and mono-graphs provide the name of the author of the work.

1. Individual author. The author is the person or body responsible for the existence of the work.

EXAMPLE

[1]Natalie Maree Belting, Kaskaskia Under the French Regime (New Orleans: Polyanthos, 1975), p. 82.

a. Fullness of name. Normally entered in the way the author is readily identified. The full name of the author should be found on the title page.

32

John Bennett Boddie, not J.B. Boddie

John Frederick Dorman, not John F. Dorman

    b. <u>Titles, offices, etc.</u> Titles of nobility, high rank and courtesy may be included. Titles of address (Mrs. Herr, etc.), <u>titles</u> of minor ranks, academic and <u>professional</u> <u>titles</u> (professor, doctor, etc.) are <u>gen-</u> <u>erally</u> ommitted. Such information should be included when it aids in distinction of persons of similar names.

EXAMPLE

    Robert Smith

    Gen. Robert Smith

Should the title page include any genea-logically significant official, academic or <u>professional</u> titles held by the author, these <u>may</u> be included after the name. Such titles as "C.G." (Certified Genealogist), "A.G." (Accredited Genealogist), and "F.A.S.G." (Fellow of the American Society of Genealo-gists) have special significance in the field of genealogy.

EXAMPLE

[1]Winston De Ville, F.A.S.G.,
Opelousas (Cottonport, La.: Polyanthos,
1973), p. 83.

c. Married women. Normally a married wo-
man's name is given as follows:

EXAMPLE

[1]Katie-Prince Ward Esker, comp.,
South Carolina Memorials I (Cottonport,
La.: Polyanthos, 1973), p. 13.

Exceptions may be under such special con-
ditions as:

1. After her marriage the author continues
   to use the name under which she is better known as a writer.

2. An author resumed a maiden name after a
   divorce and prefers to be known by that
   name.

3. The author has married a second time
   but retains the surname of her first
   husband in her capacity as a writer.

The title of address *Mrs.* is not used unless the use of her husband's name is
essential.

EXAMPLE

Mrs. John Bennett Boddie

The title of address *Ms.* is likewise never used.

2. Joint authors. If the book has two or more authors, give full names of each in order as they appear on the title page. If more than two authors are given, each full name is followed by a comma. The word "and" should be used before the name of the last mentioned author.

EXAMPLE

[1]Reba Shrophshire Wilson and Betty Shropshire Glover, The Lees and Kings of Virginia and North Carolina 1636-1976 (Ridgely, Tenn.: Wilson and Glover Publishing Co., 1975), p. 3.

3. Corporate author. A corporate body such as a genealogical society, governmental agency, city, county, or state may be the author.

EXAMPLE

[1]Mississippi Genealogical Society, Survey of Mississippi Court Houses (Jackson: By the Society, P.O. Box 5301, Jackson, Miss., 1957), p. 97.

4. <u>Anonymous works</u>. When a book does not provide the name of the author, a blank line
begins the reference. If this is the case,
but the name of the author is definitely
known, the author's name should be placed
in brackets and placed before the title as
usual.

Note that a comma always follows the name
of the author information.

<u>EXAMPLE</u>

[1]
          , <u>My Jones Family</u>
(Mobile: River Press, 1919), p. 14.

[2][John D.J.K. Jones], <u>My Jones
Family</u> (Mobile: River Press, 1919),
p. 14.

5. <u>Editor, compiler, or translator</u>. The name
of the author followed by the appropriate
designation: ed. (editor), comp. (compiler),
or trans. (translator) is preferred for all
serial publications because it can be as-
sumed that the editor, compiler, or translator may change from time to time.

6. <u>Named series and multivolume works</u>. A
series is different from, but similar to, a

multivolume work. When an individual book is part of several volumes relating to the same subject, it is often simply a multivolume work. Usually, all volumes have the same title and often the same author, compiler, or editor. If not, a comprehensive title and a general editor is found. Each book of a multivolume work will have a volume number. It is most important that the volume number of a multivolume work follow the title.

EXAMPLE

[1]Folks Huxford, F.A.S.G., comp., Pioneers of Wiregrass, Georgia, VII (Homerville, Ga.: By the comp., 1975), p. 310.

Reference style is different between a series and a multivolume work. Actually, the chief difference in the two is the publication plan. Researchers must distinguish the type of publication plan by their reference citation.

Occasionally, publishers, genealogical societies, or governmental agencies will sponsor a named series. Such a series is generally an ongoing project, whereby individual books on a related topic — often with different titles and authors — become part of a series and are given numbers. When citing a book from such a series, the name of the series and the number of the individual book are given in a first complete reference note following the title of the work.

EXAMPLE

[1]Grant Foreman, <u>Indian Removal: The Emigration of the Five Civilized Tribes</u> in the series <u>The Civilization of the American Indian</u>, No. 2 (2d ed.; Norman: The University of Oklahoma Press, 1969), p. 51.

Some books may name, in addition to the author, an editor, a compiler, or translator. The function of such a named person should be identified by abbreviating it, such as "trans." for translator, and the full name presented. This information follows the complete title and is set off by commas.

EXAMPLE

[1]Pierre Durye, <u>Genealogy: An Introduction to Continental Concepts</u>, trans. by Wilson Ober Clough, (1st English ed., New Orleans: Polyanthos, 1977), p. 83.

Sometimes the work of an author is found in a collected work with a general title and editor. It is important to know the actual author of a genealogical work. Notice that the work of the author is set in quotation marks and is not underlined in this case.

EXAMPLE

[1]Russell B. Patch, "Pitts of Georgia and Alabama" in Historical Southern Families, XIX, ed. by Mrs. John Bennett Boddie, (Baltimore: Genealogical Publishing Co., 1974), pp. 156-172.

Often, researchers engage professionals to edit genealogical work for publication. In such a case the editor may be presenting information collected, compiled, or authored by another. A reference should include such information.

EXAMPLE

[1]Chris H. Bailey, ed., Highsmiths in America, comp. by Annette Paris Highsmith (Provo: Gendex Corp., 1971), p. 100.

B. Complete Title. Give the full title as you find it on the title page of the book. Underline

39

(to indicate italics) the complete title of a published book. Because subtitles often reveal the true contents of the book, be sure to include the subtitle, also underlined, even if it is necessary to add punctuation marks.

EXAMPLE

[1]E. Stuart Gregg, Jr., comp., A Crane's Foot: (or Pedigree) of Branches of the GREGG, STUART, ROBERTSON, DOBBS, and Allied Families. (Columbia, S.C.: The R.T. Bryan Company, 1975), p. 87.

In some cases, books used will not conform to the four basic information facts. Some books are the published work of one author and a different editor, compiler, or translator. This information should be provided in a reference when necessary. Further, a researcher must give special attention to books which are parts of larger multivolume works or are a part of a specially named series. When taking information from the title page, look for other information that will indicate more complex citation needs. Most such special information will follow the title.

C. <u>Publication Facts</u>. Facts about the publication of a book always include the place, publisher, and date. When necessary, the edition is given. If any edition other than the first is cited, the edition used should be stated. Because genealogical references so seldom refer to a multivolume work as a whole, a reference to the number of volumes printed is not always necessary. Publication facts are placed in proper order: 1. edition number (if not the first), 2. place of publication 3. publisher, and 4. date — and they are placed together in parentheses. Punctuation within the parentheses is discussed below.

1. <u>Edition</u>. If the edition of the book is any other than the first, this information should be given as the first item in the order of publication facts enclosed in the parentheses. If a first edition of a book is used, no reference to the edition is necessary, and it is understood that a first edition is cited. However, a "revised" first edition should be cited, "1st ed. rev." Follow edition information with a semicolon ("2 nd ed.;").

EXAMPLE

[1]George B. Everton, Sr., and Gunnar
Rasmuson, The Handy Book for Genealogists
(3rd ed.; Logan, Utah: Everton Publishers,
1957), p. 3.

2. Place of Publication. This information will
    probably be found on the copyright page,
    although it should be included on the title
    page of a book. "Place of publication" re-
    fers to the city where the book was pub-
    lished or where the publisher has his main
    office. If the city is not well known, also
    give the state, using a standard abbreviation.

EXAMPLE

[1]E. Kay Kirkham, The Land Records of
America and their Genealogical Value (Salt
Lake City: Deseret Book Co., 1964), p. 10.

When the book does not disclose the place
of publication, use "n.p." which means "no
place" is given.

EXAMPLE

[1]Charles Fleming McIntosh, Brief
Abstracts of Lower Norfolk County and
Norfolk County Wills (Va.) 1637-1710
(n.p.: Colonial Dames of America in
the State of Virginia, 1914), p. 75.

3. <u>Publisher</u>. The name of the publisher of a book is always given as part of the publication facts in a first reference. A short form of the publisher's name and abbreviations may be used. For example, "Genealogical Publishing Company, Inc." may be shortened and abbreviated to "Genealogical Publishing Co." However, many researchers prefer to use the name of the publisher exactly as it appears in the book — and this is acceptable. Whichever way is chosen, be sure to be consistent.

EXAMPLE

[1]Katie-Prince W. Esker, ed. <u>The Genealogical Department: Source Records from the DAR magazine, 1947-1950</u> (Baltimore: Genealogical Publishing Co., 1975), p. 23

If no publisher's name appears in the book use "n. pub." to mean "no publisher"given.

EXAMPLES

[1]Richard S. Lackey, <u>Lackey Family History</u> (Forest, Miss. n. pub., 1938), p.4.

[2]Richard S. Lackey, <u>Lackey Family</u>

<u>History</u> (Forest, Miss.: By the author,
P.O. Drawer 389, 1958), p. 4.

4. <u>Date</u>. The date of publication is always an
    important publication fact. The date will
    be found on the title page or the copyright
    page.

EXAMPLE

[1]Odis Mae Spivey Dunagin, <u>Dunagin</u>
<u>Family and Allied Lines</u> (n.p.: n. pub.,
1974), p. 29.

If no date of publication can be found use
"n.d." to mean "no date."

EXAMPLE

[1]Eva Loe McDuffie, <u>The Gatlin Family</u>
<u>in America</u> (Oak Ridge, La.: n.pub., n.d.),
p. 3.

Since genealogists almost always cite a
specific volume of a multivolume work, the
date used should refer to the volume used.

EXAMPLE

[1]William S. Prince, Jr., ed., <u>The Colo-</u>
<u>nial Records of North Carolina</u> (Second
Series), V, (Raleigh: Division of Archives
and History, 1974), p. 207.

If a reprint of an earlier imprint is being used, that information should be noted. Researchers must distinguish between a reprint and a revised or second edition. Notice that in the following example, the book used was a 1974 reprint of the 1931 publication.

EXAMPLE

[1]Ellen Goode Winslow, History of Perquimans County (1931, Rpt. Baltimore: Regional Publishing Co., 1974), p. 7.

D. Page Number(s). The final basic informational fact given in a reference is the page number(s). This number refers to the specific and exact page or pages in the book on which the information cited is found. The abbreviation "p." meaning page or "pp." meaning pages should be used before the number. The arabic number(s) should be given and followed by a period. Do not use *passim* in a reference for genealogical work.

EXAMPLE

[1]Ted O. Brooke, comp., In the Name of God, Amen: Georgia Wills 1733-1860 (An Index), (Atlanta: Pilgrim Press, 1976), pp. 30-31.

II. SERIALS

Serials may be defined as publications issued in successive parts at intervals. Note should be made that a serial differs from a multivolume work and a named series. Many libraries will bind issues of a complete volume of a serial which may resemble a volume in a named series of a multivolume work, and care must be taken to observe the difference. The two major types of serials used by genealogists are: A. Periodicals and B. Newspapers.

A. __Periodicals.__ The publication plan for most genealogical periodicals is quarterly. Each issue is usually identified by the month issued (such as, January, April, July, October) or by the season (Spring, Summer, Fall, Winter). Each issue is usually numbered, and a stated number of issues constitutes a volume. Many genealogical periodicals publish articles or record abstracts in installments that may run for several issues or volumes.

__The Entry for a Periodical.__ The first complete reference for notes for an item from a periodical should include the following basic information given in the following order: 1. name of author(s), 2. title of the article, 3. name of the periodical, 4. volume of the periodical, 5. month/season and year issued, and 6. page number(s).

1. <u>Name of author(s)</u>. The basic rules for supplying the name(s) of the author also apply for author's names given in a reference to a periodical.

EXAMPLE

[1]Virginia Pope Livingston, F.A.S.G., "Some Migrations from Virginia into North Carolina," <u>The North Carolina Genealogical Society Journal</u>, III (November 1977), p. 230.

2. <u>Title of the article</u>. The title of the article is placed in quotation marks following the name of the author.

EXAMPLE

[1]Lawrence K. Wells, "William Henry of Henry's Knob," <u>The South Carolina Magazine of Ancestral Research</u>, IV (Winter 1976), p. 24.

3. <u>Name of the periodical</u>. The name of the periodical is underlined. Because some periodicals have unusual titles and may be very difficult to locate, the researcher

may place additional information in parentheses following the title.

[1]Ora Strom, "Use of Libraries,"
Rogue Digger (Rogue Valley Genealogical
Society, Ashland, Oregon), 10 (Spring-
Summer 1974), p. 88.

4. The volume of the periodical. The volume
number of the periodical follows the title.

EXAMPLE

[1]Prentiss Price, "Will of George
Dabney, King William County, Virginia,
1729" The Virginia Genealogist, 21 (Oct.-
Dec. 1977), pp. 307-310.

5. Month/season and year issued. The month/
season and year issued follow the volume
number, enclosed in parentheses.

EXAMPLES

[1]Milton Rubincam, F.A.S.G., F.N.G.S.,
"Pitfalls in Genealogical Research," Nation-
al Genealogical Society Quarterly, XLIII
(June 1955), p. 41.

or

[1]Milton Rubincam, F.A.S.G., F.N.G.S.,

"Pitfalls in Genealogical Research," <u>NGSQ</u>, XLIII (June 1955), p. 41.

6. <u>Page numbers</u>. Always include the page number(s) on which the specific information is found. The importance of including the exact page number(s) should be obvious. However, too often genealogists fail to provide the specific page number(s) to which the note refers.

EXAMPLE

[1]Kip Sperry, A.G., "Professionalism Examined," <u>Genealogical Journal</u>, 6 (June 1977), p. 59.

B. <u>Newspapers</u>.

<u>The Entry</u>. A first reference to a newspaper will probably differ slightly from a standard note for other periodicals. The following elements should be used by genealogists when citing a reference from a newspaper: 1. Name of the newspaper (place of publication — optional), 2. Date of the issue, 3. Page numbers as well as section and column numbers if considered necessary, and 4. (optional) Location.

EXAMPLE

[1]Disseminator (Brandon, Rankin Co., Miss.) 21 Feb. 1844, p. 2; Miss. Dept. of Archives & History, Jackson.

1. Name of the newspaper (place of publication optional). The name of the newspaper should be followed by the place of publication if that information is not included in a most meaningful manner in the title. The place of publication should be placed in parentheses following the title.

EXAMPLE

[1]Weekly Aurora (Paulding, Jasper Co., Miss.), 10 July 1844, p. 3; Meridian Public Library, Meridian, Miss.

2. Date of the issue. The date of the issue must be included.

EXAMPLE

[1]Southern Luminary (Jackson, Hinds Co., Miss.) 17 Aug. 1824, p. 1; Miss. Dept. of Archives & History, Jackson.

3. Page Number(s). Always include the page number on which the specific information

may be found. It may also be wise, especially in larger newspapers, to identify and
provide section numbers and column numbers.

EXAMPLE

[1]Macon Beacon (Macon, Noxubee Co.,
Miss.) 23 Oct. 1875, p. 1, col. 2; Miss.
Dept. of Archives & History, Jackson.

4. (Optional) Location. Although it will per-
haps not always be necessary, many genealogists will probably find it convenient also
to provide the location of the newspaper.
Since genealogists often consult rare newspapers, copies of which may be difficult to
locate, this information would make it
easier for the record to be examined by
the readers.

EXAMPLE

[1]Lauderdale Republican (Meridian,
Lauderdale Co., Miss.) 3 Jan. 1854, p. 3,
Ala. Dept. of Archives & History, Mont-
gomery.

instead of

[2]Lauderdale Republican (Meridian,
Lauderdale Co., Miss.) 3 Jan 1854, p. 3.

With the second reference without the location, the reader (and maybe the writer) would have to search for the location of a copy of the newspaper. One can quickly see that location information can be helpful.

EXAMPLES

[1] Clarion Ledger (Jackson, Hinds Co., Miss.) 1 Nov. 1898, p. 2, col. 2; Miss. Dept. of Archives & History, Jackson.

[2] New York Times, 3 April 1979, Sec. A, p. 4, col. 3.

[3] Dixie Times (Forest, Scott Co., Miss.) 4 Oct. 1941, p. 1, col. 1; Office of the Chancery Clerk, Scott Co. Courthouse, Forest, Miss.

[4] _____, (? pencil note 10 June 1851), newspaper clipping, original owned by John Doe, Rt. 4, Box 10, Hot Coffee, Miss.; photocopy in possession of author.

[5] Weekly Southern Conservative (n.p.) 10 Jan. 1802, p. 1, col. 1 (?); torn original owned by Richard Roe, Coldwater Plantation, Pushmataha, Miss.

III. UNPUBLISHED DOCUMENTS

The majority of sources cited by genealogists will ideally consist of references to original unpublished documents and manuscripts. Because of the great variety of such sources utilized by modern genealogists, it seems impractical to attempt to consider anything other than a suitable broad standard form. In all cases, it will be necessary for the genealogist to use good judgement in citing original documents. Because of the frequent use of some documents by genealogists, detailed considerations will be given to the following: A. Basic Form for Miscellaneous Unpublished Documents, B. Census Records, C. Tax Lists, D. Family Bibles, E. Letters, F. Civil Vital Records, G. Court House Records, H. Church Records, I. Federal Land Records, J. Military and Veteran Benefit Records, and K. Oral Interviews.

A. Basic Form for Miscellaneous Unpublished Documents. Most unpublished documents can be cited according to this basic suggested form. The following items of information should be included in the following order: 1. Descriptive title of the document, 2. Significant dates or numbers, 3. Specific location of the document used, and 4. Form used and/or repository.

1. <u>Descriptive title of the document</u>. This title will refer to the specific original record or document used. In most cases it will be up to the individual genealogist to write a descriptive title, although a few individual records may be titled. Obviously, titles selected by different genealogists will vary considerably. For example, one might wish to title a local land record transfering title to real property simply as "Deed." Another might wish to title such a record in a more detailed manner: "Deed from Andrew Meade of Nansemond Co., Va., to Jonathan Tart of Dobbs Co., N.C." Keep in mind that the title should be descriptive, and the genealogist should be consistent with information selected for an individual title of similar records.

EXAMPLE

[1]"Petition to the Legislative Council by Inhabitants Living on the Chickasawhay [River]," 16 Dec. 1808, Legislative Records (R.G. 5), Box No. 26, Territorial Archives, Miss., Dept. of Archives & History, Jackson.

2. <u>Significant date(s) or numbers</u>. Again, the individual genealogist will have to use judgement when providing a date or dates. If one date is given, it is presumed to be the date the document was completed, executed, or signed. If more than one date is shown, an explanation of all dates should be provided. The judgement of the genealogist will govern — depending on the document and the desire of the genealogist to provide detailed dates. For example, one may wish simply to provide the date a deed was signed. It would be possible to provide this date as well as the date it was acknowledged/proved and/or the date recorded. However, these dates must be explained. Remember, the individual genealogist should be consistent with information provided. If no date is found, put "n.d.," meaning "no date."

EXAMPLE

[1]"Draft map of the Settlements, on the W. side of Tombeckby [sic] R. & east [side of] the Tansaw [sic]," [with two lists of houses along the rivers on the face of the map], n.d., Manuscript and Annotated Maps of Alabama, No. W,

Cartographic Records, General Land Office (R.G. 49), National Archives, and Record Service, Washington, D.C., photocopy of original in possession of writer.

3. <u>Specific location of the document</u>. This information is very important, and care should be taken in providing it. A specific original record may be located in only one place — and not always in the most logical location. Ask the question: "Where did I find this record?" or "Where can I find this record again?" Then, answer that question in detail. A record might be found on a certain page in a numbered bound volume which is part of a multivolume official record series (Duplin Co., N.C. Deed Book 6, p. 134), or it might be found in a numbered file drawer in a lettered folder (Montgomery Co., Ala. Probate File Drawer 83, File D, Number 18). It might be located in a record group or series in the collection of a state agency (Record Group 28, N.C. Secretary of State, Box 68, Folder 16). Remember to try to answer in detail any question about the location of the specific record.

EXAMPLE

[1]"Sale of the personal property
of the Estate of Robert Massengill,"
23 March 1809, Johnston County, North
Carolina, Inventories, Settlements
Sales of Estates, Wills, 1781-1868,
Vol. 5, pp. 129-132, File No. 56.516.5,
N.C. Division of Archives & History,
Raleigh, photocopy in possession of
the writer.

4. _Form used and/or repository_. Actually, the
purpose of this information is to provide
the reader with facts that ensure easy access to the specific document cited. The
fact that many original records are available on microfilm is one reason the genealogist should provide the information about
the form of the document used. For example,
if a document from records of the Bureau of
Indian Affairs (Record Group 75) was obtained and cited from National Archives
Microfilm Publication M-234, Roll 195, in
addition to the standard citation, one would
indicate the form simply: "National Archives Publication M234, Roll 195." If the
original document was examined at the National Archives, then the Record Group, box
or volume, and a reference to the National
Archives should be given. Generally, it

would not be necessary to provide the location of the microfilm if the publisher, name, and number of the film are given. Such microfilms are widely available as are most National Archives microfilms.

EXAMPLE

[1]"Chunkyville, Lauderdale County, Mississippi Postmaster Appointments," 13 Sept. 1859, Record of Appointments of Postmasters, Vol. 25B (ca. 1857-1875), p. 386, National Archives Microfilm Publication M-841, Roll 68.

If microfilm is not used, the genealogist should always supply the name of the repository, the division (if it applies), and at least the city. Some genealogists will be generous and provide the street or mailing address of the repository.

If microfilm is not used, nor the original repository consulted, the genealogist should explain the form of record used (usually a photocopy) and provide information about the repository, generally with an address.

A repository may be an individual. Information, as complete as possible, should be provided so that the reader has ready access to the record.

[1]"Account Book of Rosehill Plantation, Hinds County, Mississippi," 1840-1846, original owned by John Doe, 5157 South River Street, Clinton, Miss. Photocopy examined at Clinton Public Library, Clinton, Miss.

B. Census Records.

The entry. A reference citation to a census report is always important because of the unique value these records hold for genealogists. Such a first reference should include: 1. A specific descriptive title, 2. Civil division information, 3. Page number and/or other specific designation, and 4. Location and/or form of record used.

EXAMPLE

[1]1850 U.S. Census (Free Schedule), Newton Co., Miss.; p. 403, family 304, dwelling 208, lines 16-18; National Archives Microfilm M-408, Roll 315.

1. A specific descriptive title. The researcher may use some discretion as to the descriptive title used. For example, "Special Schedule of the Eleventh (United States) Census (1890) Enumerating Union

Veterans and Widows of Union Veterans of the Civil War" is a descriptive title used by the National Archives to identify a certain census. Some would suggest that it would be best to identify that schedule with such a title for the first reference. Others would prefer to use a shortened title such as "1890 Special U.S. Census of Union Widows and Veterans of the Civil War." Both titles would describe the contents of the schedule. However, note that a title description "1890 Census" does *not* describe the schedules. The title selected for a census must be specific in order to be descriptive. **Also, be consistent!**

EXAMPLES

[1]1850 U.S. Census (Slave Schedule), Jasper Co., Miss.; p. 79, Line 25, National Archives Microfilm M-432, Roll 385.

[2]1837 State of Miss. Census, Kemper Co., Miss.; p. 25, Line 18, Series F (Records of the Secretary of State), Vol. 103, Miss. Dept. of Archives and History, Jackson.

2. <u>Civil division information</u>. The main basis used to establish subdivisions for a census

is to divide and arrange by civil jurisdiction. A census reference should include this necessary information. The name of the county as well as the state or territory enumerated is always necessary. Also, other civil division information would likely include subdivision facts such as the name of a city and/or ward or a town or township name or number.

EXAMPLE

[1]1840 U.S. Census, Jasper Co., Miss. (Paulding, Township 11N), p. 177, Line 29, National Archives Microfilm M-704, Roll 214.

3. Page number and/or other specific designation. Most references to census reports will at least have page references. Depending upon the report used, other designations may be needed also. For example, a family number, dwelling number, or house number may be included; and these numbers should be clearly identified in the reference. Further, genealogists who wish to provide such detailed information may desire to include line numbers. The purpose of such a detail would inform exactly which

name(s) was considered, and this can be
quite important to the genealogist.

EXAMPLE

[1]1840 U.S. Census, Jasper Co., Miss.
(Paulding, Township 11N), p. 177, Line
27, National Archives Microfilm M-704,
Roll 214.

4. <u>Location and/or form of record used.</u> This
    final item of information used in a census
    record is important. If a location is
    cited, as in the note below, the reader
    knows that the original schedule was exam-
    ined and he knows the location. If, how-
    ever, a National Archives Microfilm publi-
    cation number and roll number are given,
    the reader learns that the original sched-
    ule was not examined. In referring to a
    census in this manner, considerable — and
    sometimes important — information is pro-
    vided. Some genealogists may prefer to
    provide information regarding the location
    of the original record as well as informa-
    tion about the form of the record used.

EXAMPLE

[1]1850 U.S. Census (Free Schedule),

Newton Co., Miss.; p. 403, Family 304,
Dwelling 208, Lines 16-18;[National
Archives Microfilm M-408, Roll 315]
U.S. Bureau of the Census (R.G. 29),
MS Vol VI, National Archives and
Records Service, Washington, D.C.

C.   Tax Lists.

The entry. A reference note for a tax list
should include essentially the same information
provided for census records and should follow
about the same form. A first reference for a
tax list should include the following: 1. A
specific descriptive title, 2. Civil division
information, 3. Page number and/or other specific designation, and 4. Location and/or form
of record used.

EXAMPLES

[1]1807 Tax List (Real and Personal
Property), Baldwin Co., Ga., Capt. Bennett's
Dist., 4th Dist., p. ?, Line 4, Microfilm
Collection, Ga. Dept. of Archives & History,
Atlanta.

[2]1835 Tax List (Real and Personal
Property), Scott Co., Miss., p. 1, Line
5, Record Series G (State Auditor's
Records), Vol. 84, Miss. Dept. of
Archives & History, Jackson.

D.   Family Bible Records.

The entry. A Bible family record provides genealogists with an important source of information. Although it applies to all records, one should be especially careful to note information about a Bible properly. The fact that most Bible records are in private hands increases the danger of such records being lost or unavailable to future researchers. A first reference note for a Bible should include the following information: 1. Name and principal residences (if known) of original owner(s); 2. Publication information, including title, city, publisher, and date of publication; 3. Present owner's name and address, if known (may be a public/private agency or library); and 4. Form used (with note if necessary) and location.

EXAMPLE

[1]Family Bible Record of Alexander Gordon of Clarke Co., Miss. The Holy Bible, Containing the Old and New Testaments, Translated out of the Original Tongues and With the Former Translations Diligently Compared and Revised, (New York: D. & G. Brace, 1811), owner (1977) Mrs. Frank York, 410 Naples Rd., Jackson, Miss. 39206. Original record was hand copied, appeared authentic, and the family record, dim with age, unaltered. In possession of the writer.

One cannot always conform exactly to the standard basic form suggested. For example, sometimes the researcher does not have access to the original Bible, and this and related facts should be noted.

EXAMPLES

[1]Family Bible Record of Eleazor Biggs of Newton Co., Miss. The New Testament of Our Lord and Saviour Jesus Christ Translated out of The Original Greek and With the Former Translations Diligently Compared and Revised, (Philadelphia: Jesper Harding & Son, 1859), owner (6 June 1968), Mrs. James A. Biggs, 300 North Pearl Street, Natchez, Miss. 39120; photocopies supplied by mail to author by owner. In possession of the writer.

[2]Family Bible Record of William Clayton of Orangeburg Co., S.C., and Green and Lauderdale Cos., Miss. Location of original Bible remains unknown after inquiry; a notation on the handwritten copy was made in 1924, "accurately from the entries in a small family Bible which my wife brought this day from Heidleburg" (Jasper Co., Miss.). This Bible was printed in Edinburgh, Scotland, in 1806, and on the inside of the front cover appear the words in ink: "William Clayton — His book bought August 15, yr. 1808." The notation and copy were made by Judge Stone Deavours of Laurel, Miss. The handwritten copy of original was owned (1963) by W. M. Deavours, 407 Oak St.,

Laurel, Miss. 30441. Photocopy of
handwritten copy made by author.
In possession of the writer.

From these examples, one should see the importance of providing the reader with enough information to evaluate the record cited and locate
the record used by the researcher. The researcher should keep these suggestions in mind
when writing notes citing Bible records.

E. Letters.

The entry. The following information in the
following sequence should be included: 1. A
description of the letter, 2. The date, 3. The
specific location of the letter, and 4. The
form used and/or repository. A simple letter
citation may appear as below.

EXAMPLE

[1]John Doe to author, 16 April 1971.
Original in possession of the writer.

1. A description of the letter. The descrip-
    tion of a letter should include the names of
    of both correspondents.

[1]"George S. Gaines to Lemuel Henry,"
1 May 1812, St. Stephens, Ala., (Land Office) Registers and Receivers, Vol. 6,
115-118, Records of the General Land Office, Division D (Administrative Records),
R.G. 49, National Archives and Records
Services, Washington, D.C.

2. The date. The date of the letter should
    follow the specific title.

[1]John Doe to author, 16 Jan.
1970. Original in possession of writer.

3. The specific location of the letter.

[1]John Doe to Richard Roe, 1 March
1810, Territorial Archives, Legislative
Records, R.G. 5, Box 26, File 3, Letter
2, Miss. Dept. of Archives & History,
Jackson.

4. Form used and/or repository.

[1]"John Doe to Richard Roe," (Spring?)

1878, typed copy owned by John Smith, 418 Riverview, Gulf City, Miss., location of original unknown, portions copied in "John Smith to Author," 1 Feb. 1980. In possession of writer.

F. <u>Civil Vital Records</u>. The importance of civil records of births, deaths, marriages, and divorces to a genealogical investigation is well known to researchers. Because official civil vital records may be obtained from a local or state agency, location of the document in the citation is very important. Further, care should be taken to distinguish between a civil record, a church record, or a private record when documenting a birth, death, marriage, or divorce.

<u>The entry</u>. The following basic information should be included in the following order: 1. Descriptive title, 2. Significant dates and/or numbers, 3. Specific location of the document, and 4. The form used and/or repository.

EXAMPLE

[1]Birth Certificate for John Doe, 10 June 1920, File No. 6837-20, Mississippi State Board of Health, P.O. Box 1700, Jackson, Miss. 39205. Certified copy in possession of writer.

G. Courthouse Records. The county courthouse will be the source of many records for the genealogist. Special care must be taken when citing records from books of deeds, wills, estates, inventories, marriages, court records, minutes, marks and brands, etc.

The entry. The following information should be given in the following order for most court house records: 1. Descriptive title of the record, 2. Significant dates, 3. Specific location of the record, and 4. Form used and/or repository.

1. Descriptive title. The researcher should describe exactly the document being used.

EXAMPLE

[1]"Deed of Sale from Jacob Blount to Henry Warren," 18 Jan. 1775 (recorded March 1775), Craven County, N.C., Deed Bk 22, pp. 12-13, N.C. State Library, County Core Collection Microfilm No. 84-21.

2. Significant dates. Following the descriptive title, all significant dates should be given. The date the document was written should always be given first.

EXAMPLE

[1]Mortgage from John Doe to Richard Roe, 4 Jan. 1920 (acknowledged 4 Jan. 1920, recorded 7 Jan. 1920, cancelled 2 Jan. 1921), Gulf Co., Miss., Deed of Trust Bk 4, pp. 416-417, Office of the Chancery Clerk, Court House, Gulf City, Miss. Certified copy in possession of the writer.

3. Specific location of the record. Because records are not always located in the place a knowledgeable researcher would expect to find them, the specific location of a record should be given.

EXAMPLE

[1]"John Doe marriage bond to Jane Roe, Craven Co., N.C.," 10 March 1789, original owned by Richard Smith, 410 Riverview, Gulf City, Miss.

4. Form used and/or repository. Because many original court house records are now located in state repositories, it is quite important to include the repository and the form used.

EXAMPLE

[1]"Will of John Doe," 18 May 1816, Gulf Co., Miss., Will Book I, pp. 400-402,

Miss. Dept. of Archives & History,
Jackson. Photocopy of original in
possession of writer.

H.   Church and Cemetery Records. Church and cemetery records may vary considerably, depending
upon the type of record and denomination.

The entry. A first reference note for a church
and cemetery record should follow the following
standard form: 1. Descriptive title, 2. Significant dates, 3. Specific location, and 4. Form
used and/or repository.

1.   Descriptive title. The researcher should
provide some title for the specific record
consulted.

EXAMPLES

- Membership list
- Death record for John Doe
- Marriage record for John Doe and Mary Roe
- Birth record for Jane Doc
- Baptism record for Richard Roe
- Minutes of the monthly (weekly) meeting

2.   Significant dates. Any significant date
should be added to the citation. Sometimes
the date of the event and the date of the
recording of the event will be different.

EXAMPLE

[1]"Baptism Record for John Doe,"
born 14 June 1815, Baptized 15 June 1815,
St. Mary's Catholic Church Misc. Bk II,
p. 182, Gulf City, Ala. Photocopy sent
author by Richard Roe, 180 River St.,
Gulf City, Ala.

3. Specific location. It is always very important to give the specific location of a
record by volume or book number. Also,
when citing a cemetery marker, the location
of the cemetery should be provided.

EXAMPLES

[1]Headstone inscription for George
Massengill, Fellowship Cemetery, Jasper
Co., Miss. (S. 14, T. 4N – R. 13E, Choc-
taw Principle Meridian). Author's visit
10 June 1970.

[2]Headstone inscription for Nathan
Smith, Lot No. 17, Smith Cemetery, Con-
cord, Mass. (1 mile west of city limits
on State Route No. 82). Author's visit
1 July 1927.

4. Form used and/or repository. It is always
necessary to provide the name of the repository of a record. Readers can assume the
original records were consulted at the named
depository unless information to the contrary
is provided.

EXAMPLES

[1]"Membership List," 10 Aug. 1821, Goodwater Baptist Church Minute Bk. I, Church Archives, Meridian, Miss., p. 3

or

[2]"Membership List," 10 Aug. 1821, Goodwater Baptist Church Minute Bk I, Church Archives, Meridian, Miss. Photocopy of pp. 1-7 provided author by church clerk.

I. <u>State and Federal Land Records.</u> A citation for an original entry for a land record will often not be found with local deed records in court houses. Therefore, sometimes these records require special attention by genealogists. For a document of original entry for land in one of the "state land" states or in the "public land" states, the following information should be provided.

<u>The entry</u> The following information should be provided in this order: 1. A title for the particular record, 2. The type of record from which the entry was taken, 3. A statement with reference to the government agency and/or land office, 4. The specific location of the record, and 5. The form used and/or repository.

EXAMPLE

[1]"Patent of Thomas Boulton, assignee
of George Buchannan, 1 January 1849,"
Credit Entry, St. Stephens (Ala.) U.S.
Land Office, Credit Vol. 30, Misc. Vol.
136, p. 310, Bureau of Land Management,
Eastern States Office, Alexandria, Va.

1. A title for the particular record. It is
   often important to know the exact sheet of
   paper being cited so the title should be
   specific enough to direct a researcher to
   a particular paper or record in a file.

EXAMPLE

[1]"John Finlay Journal Entry," Credit
Entry, St. Stephens (Ala.) U.S. Land Office, Journal A, Vol. 1, 1800–1815,
p. 182, St. Stephens, Ala., Land Office
Bk. No. 51, Civil Archives, Ala. Dept.
of Archives and History, Montgomery.

2. The type of record from which the entry was
   taken. Because entry records of the public
   land states are filed by the type of entry,
   i.e., "cash," "credit under," "homestead,"
   etc., it is absolutely necessary to know
   the type of entry in many cases.

EXAMPLE

[1]"Original entry for Richard Roe,"
10 Feb. 1840, Cash Entry, Columbia (Miss.)
U.S. Land Office, Cash Entry File No.
18364, Washington Federal Record Center,
Suitland, Md. Photocopy in possession
of writer.

3. A statement with reference to the government agency and/or land office. Since many states and the federal government arranged records by named land offices, it is often necessary to know the exact government agency and/or land office in order to locate a cited document.

EXAMPLE

[1]"John McRae ledger account," Credit
Entry, U.S. Tract Book, St. Stephens
(Ala.), Vol 14 (W.M.L.), 5-10-5, 3751,
Augusta (Miss.) Land Office Vol. 4, No.
3947, R.G. 49, Washington National Records
Center, Suitland, Md.

4. The specific location of the record. Researchers should be very careful always to give volume and page references and/or file number references in dealing with original land record entries.

EXAMPLE

[1]"George Mashingill Land Warrant,"
N.C. State Land Warrant No. 379, Johnston
Co., N.C., File No. 3083, Secretary of
State, Raleigh, N.C.

5. The form used and/or repository. The repository holding the original record should
be given if it was seen there by the researcher. If not, the form used by the
researcher should be stated.

EXAMPLE

[1]"Houston Griffin Land Grant,"
Texas State Land Grant No. 10, Mar-
tin Co., Tex. Photocopy in Vertical
File No. 1783 (Griffin Family), Tex.
State Archives, Austin.

J. Military Records. A citation for a military
record is quite important. The most frequently
used documents of this type are, of course,
federal service records and items from federal
veteran's benefit files. Nevertheless, the
citation form below could be used for military
records for state or foreign government military service as well as for service for the
Confederate States of America.

The entry. The following information should be

76

provided in the following order: 1. A title for a particular record, 2. The file title and number, 3. A statement with reference to the government and the service, 4. The specific location of the file, and 5. The form used and/ or the repository.

EXAMPLE

[1]"Confederate Service Record for Joshua I. Dyess," Muster Roll, July 1862, Co. C, 36 Reg't Miss. Vols., Service in Army of the Conf. States of America, Misc. Conf. Rolls, Box 16, Miss. Archives & History, Jackson.

1. <u>A title for a particular record.</u> A title should be provided for the specific record which documents the statement.

EXAMPLE

[1]"Affidavit of John Pinkstaff," Andrew Pinkstaff Pension No. R8261, U.S. Revolutionary War Service, War Department Collection of Revolutionary War Records (Record Group 93), National Archives and Records Service, Washington, D.C.

2. <u>The file title and numbers.</u> Usually, many types of records are grouped in a file under the name of the soldier with the

service. This file will most often have a number following the name. Both the name and the file number should be provided, if possible.

[1]"Muster Roll of Captain Samuel Bigham's Company of South Carolina Infantry" for 29 June to 1 Sept. 1812, James Deer Compiled Military Service Record, no number, U.S., War of 1812 Service, Records of the Adjutant General (Record Group 94), National Archives and Records Service, Washington, D.C. In possession of writer.

3. A statement with reference to government and to the service. Because military service could be for the United States, any state, the Confederate States of America, or a foreign power, the name of the government should be stated. This should be followed with some reference to the service, i.e., "War of 1812," "Revolutionary War," or "Mexican War."

EXAMPLE

[1]"Muster Roll of Captain James Smith's Militia," 1 June 1862, Army of the Confederate States of America, War Between the States, p. 2, line 16,

Private collection of John Doe, 101
Gulf Road, Mobile, Ala. Copy in
possession of writer.

4. The specific location of the file. Since
   military records are generally found as
   part of a government's official archives,
   the specific reference to these records
   should be given.

EXAMPLE

[1]"Declaration of Mary Deer, widow
of James Deer," James Deer Bounty Land
File No. Bt. Wt. 25462-80-55, U.S., War
of 1812 from S.C., Records of the Veterans Administration, R.G. 15, National
Archives and Record Service, Washington,
D.C.

5. The form and/or repository. The repository
   holding the original record should be given
   if it was examined by the researcher. If
   not, the form used by the researcher should
   be stated.

EXAMPLE

[1]"Declaration of Mary Deer, Widow
of James Deer," James Deer Bounty Land
File No. Bt. Wt. 25462-80-55, U.S., War
of 1812 from S.C., Records of the Veterans Administration, R.G. 15, National

79

Archives and Records Service, Washington,
D.C. Photocopy in possession of writer,

K. Oral Interviews. The widespread use of oral interviews is well known to most researchers. Information obtained from such sources requires
special attention by genealogists.

The entry. A first reference note for an oral
interview should follow standard form: 1. Title
of notes or tapes, 2. Date of interview, 3. Interviewer, 4. Present owner's name and address,
5. Form used and location, and 6. Evaluation information (optional).

1. Title. The title should include the name
of the person being interviewed. In short,
title your notes or tapes.

EXAMPLE

[1]"Oral interview with John Doe,"
13 September 1968, by Richard Roe, recording owned by author, Gulf City,
Miss. John Doe was living in Mobile,
Ala., on 10 June 1920 and was about 16
years old.

2. Date of interview. The date of the interview should be provided, if possible.

[1]"Oral interview with Richard Roe,"
11 June 1920, by John Doe, Gulf City
Public Library, Gulf City, Miss., written
interview report; interview made for news
article.

3. Interviewer. The name of the person or agency
    conducting the interview should be provided.

EXAMPLE

[1]"Interview with John Doe," 6 July
1976, by Gulf County, Mississippi Historical Society, Society Library, 814
River Street, Gulf City, Miss., tape
recording; quality of sound reproduction
very poor.

4. Present owner's name and address. The pre-
    sent owner of an oral interview, tape or
    notes, may be a public/private agency or li-
    brary. However, often the owners of oral
    interviews for genealogical purposes will be
    individuals.

EXAMPLE

[1]"Interview with Jane Roe," 10
August 1961, by author, owned by author,
Gulf City, Miss. Original tape recording
used at author's home; the great grand-
mother of Jane Roe lived in Jane Roe's
father's home until her death when Jane
Roe was 17 years old.

5. <u>Form used and location.</u> It is a general practice to transcribe oral interviews from tape recordings. The researcher should include in his citation the exact form used. If transcription is used, careful researchers will realize that possible errors could have occurred in transcribing an interview from a tape recording.

EXAMPLE

[1]"Interview with Jane Doe," n.d., by John Smith, local historian, Gulf City, Miss. Location of original tape recording unknown. Copy of transcription provided author by Richard Roe, 110 Beach Ave., Gulf City, Miss.

6. <u>Evaluation information (optional).</u> Because information obtained from oral interviews is always subject to the most careful and serious evaluation by genealogists, it may be wise to provide any special information about the interview or the person being interviewed to aid in such evaluation.

EXAMPLE

[1]"Interview with Mary Doe," 18 May 1968 by Martha Roe, transcript owned by Jane Roe, 410 Ocean Drive, Gulf City,

Miss. Telephone reading to author,
Gulf City, Miss. Mary Doe was reported in poor health at time of
interview. Martha Roe asked questions,
but also provided Mary Doe with certain
promptive information. It appears that
Mary Doe simply responded "yes" to almost any question asked her.

PART III

SHORT OR SECOND USE OF NOTES

SHORT OR SECOND USE OF NOTES

As observed, the first time a reference note appears it must always be presented in complete form. However, when a second or subsequent reference is made to a note which has been cited in full form, a short citation may be employed. Never use a short form as a first reference to a work. The circumstances will determine the proper shortened form.

A. Short Title References. A reference to a work previously fully cited, but *not* immediately following the citation in full form should use the short title form. Information should include: 1. The last name or surname only of the author, 2. A short form of the title, and 3. The page number(s).

EXAMPLE

First complete form:

[1]Bill R. Linder, How to Trace Your Family History (New York: Everest House, 1978), p. 18.

Short Form:

[2]Linder, Family History, p. 18.

1. The surname only of the author. The author's first-name initials or first name should not

be given in a short form reference unless works by persons of the same surname have been previously cited in full.

EXAMPLE

[1]Helmbold, *Ancestry*, p. 168.

2. <u>A short form of the title</u>. Never use only the author and pages, but add a short title. The researcher should use good judgement in selecting key words from a title to shorten it. Avoid rearrangement of the order of words selected from a title. Anytime a short title is to be used in a later reference, the complete (first) citation should call attention to the fact and indicate it by adding: "Hereinafter cited as _____" or "Hereinafter, _____." Researchers should remember that abbreviations may be used in this manner. The use of Latin abbreviations *op. cit.* and *loc. cit.* following the author's name should not be employed by genealogists; genealogy requires preciseness.

EXAMPLES

[1]Grimes, <u>Wills</u>, p. 18.

[2]"Will of Henry Woodnot(t)," Records

of the Secretary of State, Wills 1712-
1722, Book 2, p. 176, N.C. Division
of Archives and History, Raleigh. Hereinafter referred to as N.C.D.A.H.

3. The page number(s). To indicate pages always use full numbers such as 110-180, not
   110-80.

EXAMPLE

[1]McDuffie, Gatlin Family, pp. 14-19.

B. Other Short Reference Forms. When a reference
to a work previously fully cited is immediately
preceeding, another short reference form can be
used. The Latin abbreviation *ibid.* may be used
to save space. Note that this short reference
must be to the complete citation immediately
preceeding. Further, note that *ibid.* cannot be
used to refer to a preceeding work when there
is an intervening reference.

EXAMPLES

[1]Ellen Goode Winslow, History of
Perquimons County (1931 rept. Baltimore:
Regional Publishing Co., 1974), p. 7.

[2]Ibid., p. 18.

translator 36
translator, abbreviation 28
typescript, abbreviation 28

various dates, abbrevia-
  tion 28
verso, abbreviation 28
videlicet, abbreviation 28
vital records 68
vital record, abbreviation
  28
volume of periodical 48
volume(s), abbreviation 28

Wills - see courthouse
  records

year, abbreviation 28